"O'Hara helps us find the quiet place inside us where inner peace abounds. In our harried lives it's comforting to remember the quiet place can be revisited."

—**Michele Weiner-Davis, M.S.W.**,
author of *Fire Your Shrink* and *Divorce Busting*

"There is breathtaking wisdom and strength to be found in a single moment of silence—and Nancy O'Hara offers a kind invitation to listen. FIND A QUIET CORNER is a gentle opening; it beckons us into fruitful practice. Here, we harvest the compelling grace that is born only in the quiet of our lives."

—**Wayne Muller, minister and therapist,**
author of *Thursday's Child: The Spiritual Advantages
of a Painful Childhood*

FIND A QUIET CORNER

"This simple yet profound book ought to be read by all people who live in the so-called civilized world. Civilization has deprived us of our natural condition as human beings. Nancy O'Hara offers a guide to the natural, peaceful world.

Even just reading the chapter titles is worthwhile: 'Let Your Breathing Guide You,' 'Make It a Habit,' 'Keep It Yours,' 'Turn Bad Situations to Your Advantage,' 'When Things Don't Go Your Way.' These phrases can stimulate our sincere curiosity. In our busy, everyday life, we do not pay much attention to these simple matters, hence no quiet corner. As the author says about attention, 'It is truly simple and immediately rewarding.' "

—**Eido T. Shimano**
Abbot of the Zen Studies Society
November 24, 1994
Dai Bosatsu Zendo

FIND A QUIET CORNER

A SIMPLE GUIDE
TO SELF-PEACE

NANCY O'HARA

WARNER BOOKS

A Time Warner Company

Copyright © 1995 by Nancy O'Hara
All rights reserved.

Warner Books, Inc., 1271 Avenue of the Americas, New York, NY 10020

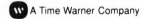 A Time Warner Company

Printed in the United States of America
First Printing: May 1995
10 9 8 7 6 5 4 3 2

Library of Congress Cataloging-in-Publication Data

O'Hara, Nancy.
    Find a quiet corner : a simple guide to self-peace / Nancy O'Hara.
        p.   cm.
    ISBN 0-446-67111-8
    1. Stress (Psychology)   2. Stress management.   3. Peace of mind.
I. Title.
BF575.S75O27   1995
158'.1'082—dc20   94-31052
                                                                CIP

Cover illustration by Linda Scharf

Cover photo by Barry Marcus

Cover design by Julia Kushnirsky

Book design by Giorgetta Bell McRee

To Dad and Donge

For bringing my attention to my breath as they lost theirs

Acknowledgments

I first wish to thank my previous employer for firing me from my job, for without that experience this book would not exist. Nor would it exist without the following people. Thanks and Gassho to Boun Nancy Berg for organizing retreats to Dai Bosatsu Zendo, introducing me to Zen practice, and congratulating me when I lost my job. Bill and Bob for creating a program that saved my life and placed me on a spiritual path. Rinaldo Petronio for being my guardian angel. Donge John Haber for his grace and humor, and for demystifying the Zen experience for me. Tim Kelley for causing me enough heartache to propel me into sitting. John Michel for his encouragement and editorial help early on, for having faith in me as a writer, and for being a friend. Betsy Lerner for her support and practical help as well as her enthusiasm for this project. Eido Shimano Roshi for opening his monastery home to me and for teaching me to breathe. Seigan Ed Glassing for teaching me so many things about acceptance. Junpo Denis Kelly for his generosity. Edra, Elly, Donna, Leslie, Susan, and Ruth for allowing me to be of service and for giving me more than I gave. Sarah Jane Freymann for her vision and assistance in shaping an early draft. Barbara Suter for getting me through many difficult years with her sense of humor and love. Tom Fuller for being a steady friend.

Introduction

I used to wish my life away. I lived my life thinking ahead to the next thing—the next day, when I had a date with so-and-so and wouldn't that be nice; the next job, because I hated my current one so much; the next year, when I was planning to take that great vacation which held the promise of changing my life; the next prince charming, who would rescue me from my life because the last one was really a frog and I was meant to be saved. I couldn't wait for the next experience that was sure to transform me and my life. I still have the tendency to live in the future, but today I notice when I do and am usually able to catch myself and bring my attention back to the moment. But it took some time and a lot of pain to shift my awareness into the present.

My journey in search of a quiet corner began with loss and a great deal of despair. It was 1985. I was living my life as usual, waiting for something to happen, retreating from myself and my world with drugs and alcohol, and living in a black hole of despair, not caring much about my life. In fact, I considered ending my life just to escape the misery. And then my father died. The shock of losing the only person in my life who seemed to love me was devastating. For a short while I sank further into despair and a haze of intoxication. But for some reason his death made it clear to me that I wanted to live. I saw how I was slowly slipping into oblivion. Some force beyond me and my ego drove me to admit that my life was a mess, and I made a decision to move toward life rather than death. I put down drugs and alcohol and began the move toward health.

Three years later, after spending much time working toward recovery, another loss forced me to recommit to my quiet corner journey. My prince charming of the moment left me, for seemingly no reason. My mind wouldn't leave me alone. My ego was crushed, my heart was bruised, and my mind blamed me. I sank into a self-deprecating state of loneliness and tortured myself with notions that it was all my fault, that I was unlovable, that I would never be happy, that I got what I deserved. The pain was debilitating and I sometimes thought I might drop off the sane world into that of the insane. That's how noisy and confused my mind was. Because I was desperate, I went on a retreat to a Zen Buddhist monastery in the Catskill Mountains. Because I always wanted to be the good student and get the gold star at the end of the day, I did what was suggested that weekend. When told to sit still during the zazen periods of meditation, I sat still. I was in so much mental pain that I would have done anything for the promise of soothing it.

The physical pain of sitting was so excruciating I was convinced that I was doing serious permanent damage to my body. But something happened that weekend in the stillness of sitting and in the encounter with pain. The physical pain took my mind off the mental pain and taught me that pain is only temporary and often simply a measure of my ego and its attachments. I continued sitting after leaving the mountain, and I went on other retreats over the next few years. My life was changing, I was changing, and the pain of that time subsided to the point where I was actually enjoying my life. By 1991 I was in a job that I loved and in a relationship that was working, and I had just purchased my first home. Life was okay.

Then the bottom fell out again. Within a month I lost my boyfriend and my job. I hadn't realized until I lost them how much my identity was wrapped up in both, especially my job. I was a very sad and broken person. The self-blaming demons returned. I didn't know what to do next, so I retreated to the monastery for a weekend to think about my next move. Beginning with that weekend and with the help of many people I started on yet another path of recovery. I had always wanted to write, and when I put forth the idea of spending more time at the monastery and writing about the experience, I was encouraged to do so by the monks and by many friends who cared about me. I lived there for five months and am changed from that experience. (That, of course, is another book.)

Find a Quiet Corner is a product of all this experience. It comes from much personal pain and the need to quiet my mind. My pattern had been not to make changes in my life unless I was in great pain and my back was up against the wall. My instinct is to continue to resist change, but today I am aware when I do this and I use the techniques in this book to accept the change that is inevitable. I am grateful that my life was filled with so much pain and that I was introduced to a form of meditation that helps me to accept and understand this pain.

While you can open to any page in this book and find inspiration, you will get the most from it by working through it from front to back, from beginning to end. I know many people who are in pain and could benefit from the suggestions in this book. If I am able to help but one other person, all my pain will have been worthwhile. But I also know that we each have our own path and unless we're ready to surrender, nothing can force us. Pain is a fact of life. Joy is available to us also, but not unless we understand the pain. I have experienced joy for the first time in my life since starting on the quiet corner path. I will continue to experience pain, but I now know that joy is also probable if I continue my quiet corner practice.

Why a Quiet Corner?

*T*his book is for those of you who haven't the time to do all those things that are expected of you every day. You've got the demands of your boss, the demands of your spouse, the demands of your children, the demands of your community, and perhaps most of all, the demands of your own personal making weighing on you. You are distracted to the point of mild insanity. You hardly have time to eat - how can you be expected to read a book, let alone find some alone time for yourself?

If you take a moment out of your hectic day and settle down with this book, you'll learn how to find some time and you'll get back in touch with your understanding of how important it is to spend some time with yourself. This book is not about adding yet one more burden to your already full-to-exploding life. It's about learning how to unburden yourself, how to *un*do some of the complications in your life and clear a path toward smoothness. While thinking of the greater good may only be a distraction just now, consider this for this moment: if our culture is to evolve, it is imperative that we each learn to take some time for ourselves on a daily basis and develop our own individual spiritual awareness. Finding a quiet corner is one way for each of us to do our part.

But the greater gain is secondary. The primary gain will be

in your daily life. And it won't take a revolution or a complete change of lifestyle to enjoy the rewards. It will take only a few small movements to reap big changes.

If you've read this far, you are already aware of your need to slow down. If you feel compelled to go further, you've already accepted this. And if you read on, you'll learn some actions you can take to introduce some calm into your life.

What Is a Quiet Corner?

A moment in time. A place in time. A breath. A quiet corner can be found anywhere, can be created anytime. It is an attitude, an outlook. It can be found in your particular approach to your particular day. A quiet corner simply needs a slight shift in perspective to emerge.

A quiet corner is the calm after a storm. Think of a morning after a snowstorm, your world buried under a foot or two of snow. Venturing outside, you may notice the effects of this blanket of white. Before the roads are plowed and cars dug out, there is no traffic noise. Most people, while perhaps dreading the shovel, are smiling and awed by the beauty of it all. You might think more carefully about each step you take. Once you've given in to this force of nature, you are in the moment aware only of your next move, not thinking of tomorrow. You can't take your usual path, you must rethink things. Your perspective shifts. You are in a quiet corner.

But it needn't take a dramatic act of nature to create a quiet corner. Once you identify this state of grace, you can learn to create it on your own. All it takes is a decision and a resignation. Give up your usual practices, leave at the door of your quiet corner all expectations, and be prepared to enter a world where anything is possible.

Breathing

This is where it all begins—and ends. The foundation of any quiet corner is breathing. If you breathe into your quiet corner and allow your breathing to direct you in your search, it will create space and quiet for your corner. As I concentrate on breathing slowly, my focus shifts and I welcome the ensuing calm as it enfolds and comforts me.

Most of us breathe very shallowly. We only breathe into our throats and don't allow oxygen deep into our bodies. Take a moment. Become aware of how you're breathing in this moment. Is your breathing deep and calm? Or is it shallow and hurried? The next time you feel stressed, panicked, or otherwise pressured, again notice your breathing patterns. Your breathing will be shallower than normal. Or you may discover that you are actually holding your breath, not breathing at all. This is a common response to stress. Think for a moment about what this might mean to your well-being.

As a simple exercise, take a breath through your nostrils and send this breath into your lower chest. Continue inhaling as you first fill up your lower chest, then your middle chest, and then your upper chest. Slowly release this breath—first the upper chest, then the middle chest, and then the lower chest. Do this three times as slowly as possible. In doing this, you will discover your first quiet corner.

If you take three deep breaths a few times during each day, especially at those critically stressful moments, you'll be on your way to reducing stress and introducing some serenity into your life. It is truly simple and immediately rewarding.

Caring about and for Yourself

As our society has become so enthralled with narcissism, many of us have come to believe that self-love is bad and selfish. We have done ourselves wrong here. There is nothing wrong with loving ourselves. In fact, this is necessary before we can truly love another. Let's try to put aside the old myths and have faith that love sent in any direction is positive and healthy.

If you've ever been on an airplane, you'll remember being told to put on your own oxygen mask in the event of an emergency, before helping young children: if you help yourself first you'll be better equipped to help others. In the same way, love yourself first. Take some time for yourself. Consider these actions to be done in the service of others. A quiet, loving corner can be the nurturing ground for your own and your family's well-being.

Love is what we all ultimately seek, but to get love we must give it. And in order to give it we need to know it for ourselves. Unless we take good care of ourselves we will have nothing to give others. Caring for ourselves is the first step in the process.

Become the Person You Already Are

*I*f you have children or have been around children you'll notice that they are often quite content and satisfied to exist in their own little world, fascinated with the particular project that at any given moment absorbs them. Whether they are playing with building blocks or digging in the sand, for a certain amount of time they need no one and want nothing. They are comfortable in their own skin and often seem to be transported to another world.

As we become adults and assume responsibilities in the world, we tend to stop this practice; we become other- and outer-directed and relegate all childhood activities to the past. When these childlike inclinations are stifled, we lose the sense of wonderment that often accompanies them. Our creativity becomes boxed up and we wonder why life has dulled. That child is still within us, though, and can be rediscovered in our quiet corner. It is there that we can once again get in touch with our true spirit.

Visit a neighborhood playground or ball field and watch children as they play. Volunteer to coach a Little League team or just observe the kids as they play and let them coach you. Allow them to teach you what it's like to be free and uninhibited. After a snowfall, make a snowman with the neighborhood kids or engage in an innocent snowball fight. Ride the waves at the ocean and delight in the freedom of it. Rake leaves into a big enough pile to hide in and have some fun. As you loosen up and begin to discover how to let go and be spontaneous, take this attitude with you into your quiet corner and nurture it there. Before long your true nature will reveal itself and some of the tension in your life will disappear.

Get to Know Yourself Again

*M*ost of us can't remember sitting in rapture as a child. Or if we can remember, we merely mourn the loss of such times and consider them over and done with. To alter our "grown-up" way of seeing we simply need the key of willingness.

Be willing to spend time alone with yourself. Look closely at who you are, what makes you laugh or cry. Let go of old encrusted notions that bog you down. Ease them out of your mind. Invite your idiosyncrasies to have their say, and keep the ones that thrill you.

As you spend more time with yourself, your view of the world will begin to change. You'll see yourself in a new light and have a new understanding of who you are in the world. Long forgotten parts of you will rise to the surface and come alive. You'll be more involved in your life than ever before, thanks to your own quiet corner.

Trust in the Process

Whenever you are stuck, breathe. If you find yourself moving too fast, breathe. As you face an important decision, breathe. Breathing is crucial to your emotional and spiritual health. Whenever there is a question in your mind about what to do next or how to do it, just breathe. Sooner or later the solution will appear. While we'd all like it sooner, we may find that later is more often the rule. And that's what makes this so hard. So many of us never give later a chance. But later always comes, if it's not sooner. So breathe and trust in the process.

Finding Your Quiet Corner

Tension and stress have an impact on our breathing, and our breath often stops at our diaphragms. We are literally cut in half by this manner of breathing, as a significant area of our body gets no oxygen. You can easily correct this and learn to breathe deep into your body, sending oxygen to your whole being. Begin with the three-part deep breathing exercises, sending your breath deep into your abdomen. As you exhale each breath, begin to count each exhalation. Focus on your breathing and nothing else.

Inhale slowly and gradually, filling up each section of your chest. Count as you exhale and let each count last the length of your exhalation: o-o-o-on-n-ne-e. Now slowly inhale again and on the next exhalation count two. Again. Inhale. Exhale. Count three. This is all it takes to begin the process. Practice this three-part, three-breath breathing every day. If you can, practice throughout the day. As you read this, remember to breathe.

When breathing remains shallow, resistance to change rises and the search for a quiet corner may never begin. Practice your breathing. You will open up. Your world will open up. You'll find corners where there once was nothing. Your awareness of your surroundings will heighten. Your outlook will change. Breathe slowly and deeply.

For a while you may only find the time to practice your breathing. That's okay. It's a beginning and it's beneficial to your peacefulness. If you are determined, your day will soon open up to include more. So breathe away.

Be Creative

*I*f your creative activity has slowed down or become dormant over time, you can slowly start nurturing it back to life as you seek your quiet corner. In fact, you'll need to engage and develop your creative juices because even though your quiet corner may be right in front of you, you'll just continue to trip over it and ignore it until you become willing to see it and use it. Creativity comes into play and touches on all aspects of your quiet corner.

"Play" is a key word here. Approach your quiet corner as you would your own personal playground. You know yourself better than anyone; you know what works best for you, what inspires and stimulates you. As your creativity reawakens, encourage it and feed it. Try not to approach your quiet corner as a chore, something that you must do to achieve something, even if that something is joy and harmony. Try to approach your quiet corner in a playful manner. Think of it as a break for enjoyment rather than work. Try not to edit your thoughts as you begin. Let your imagination run wild and nurture your creative mind. We all have creative minds, and it is in your quiet corner that you can retrieve yours.

One of my quiet corners came to me in a dream. The time before, during, and after sleep is my quiet-corner creative thinking time. I'm relaxed enough to hear my right brain and willing enough to listen.

Go gently. Let go and trust yourself as you learn to explore your creative instincts.

Morning

*E*arly morning is the perfect time to begin looking for your quiet corner. Getting up fifteen minutes to a half hour earlier than usual will give you plenty of time to spend on this new journey. And being awake before the rest of your world will add a new and peaceful dimension to your day. Simply by changing your normal patterns, your perspectives will shift. Try waking early as a new routine for a week. Then decide if it's the perfect time for your quiet corner.

If morning becomes you, the gifts waiting for you at that time of day will quickly penetrate your awareness: sound changes dramatically in the early morning; light and shadows are uniquely displayed. Both inside and outside the home everything is different. People sounds are softer as the world belongs to other life. Taking a slow stroll through your neighborhood the musical chattering of birds can be heard. Walking to a nearby park listen as the wind stirs the treetops. Sit by the water. As you breathe in the soothing quiet of early morning you'll enter your day with a new measure of calm.

Schedule a Meeting with Yourself

Although our days get so jam-packed with activity, we always seem to be able to squeeze in one more thing. A meeting with the boss or a special client. An interview with our child's teacher or caregiver. A lunch or dinner date with a special friend. Somehow we manage to get things done even though a nagging voice at the back of our brains often tells us we should do more, more, more.

Try to fit yourself into your day. Consider this appointment with yourself as your most critical one and change it only in a dire emergency. Write it in your datebook, even. Be careful, though, not to choose the most difficult time for yourself. Setting yourself up to miss this most important appointment will only lead to discouragement and delay. One day at a time decide that you are the most important date on your calendar.

Taking time for yourself is life-affirming. It will teach you that anything is possible if you continue the practice. This is just the beginning.

Physical Spaces

*C*ertain places can have amazing power over us. Anyone would agree that the Grand Canyon is a perfect place to sit in rapt silence and soak up nature's majesty. There are few places as grand as the canyon, but our environment, no matter how grand, affects us. In searching for your quiet corner be sensitive to space that in and of itself produces calm.

If you're lucky enough to have a spare room at home to designate as yours, reserve it and use it exclusively as your quiet corner. Or simply assign a corner of another room (the den, the dining room, the bedroom) and transform it into your own personal quiet corner. Include your family in this process. They might even be happy to free up some space for your corner when they see the effect it has on you. Perhaps a quiet corner could be established for each member of your family and a certain time of the day designated as quiet time for all.

If you can't find a space at home to call your own, there are many other places you can use. The back of a church when there's no service going on can be a perfect space to find your quiet corner. Before work, at lunchtime, or at the end of the day, walk into a neighborhood church, synagogue, temple, or mosque and decide if your quiet corner waits for you there.

You needn't always seek out the same place. But it does help to have one special place for those times when you have no extra energy for the search and are simply in need of some calm. After a while you'll be able to transform almost any space and retreat to the quiet corner in your mind.

Avoidance

As you begin to seek out your quiet corner and experiment with various options, you may hit a wall now and then. This is the wall of avoidance. It will seem to come from nowhere and will have great strength and persistence. It will tell you that this whole exercise is foolish, that you haven't the time for such things, that you have more important things to do, that you can do it tomorrow, and so on.

It's very normal to hit this wall. Although you may be convinced that a quiet corner is exactly what you need to find some balance in your life, it will take some persistence and determination on your part to succeed in finding your corner and holding on to it. Try hard not to allow the negative, dissuasive voices to win. But don't be surprised when they come. Just accept them. Keeping your determination to find your quiet corner is all that matters. Believe it or not, the avoidance voices will soon disappear altogether and be replaced by positive, encouraging voices, assuring you that you're on the right path as you seek your quiet corner.

Lunch Break

While you may be the type to eat on the run, at your desk or not at all, the lunch hour is an ideal time to set aside for your quiet corner. Even if you have Scrooge for a boss, or if you are your own Scrooge, no one will begrudge you time off to eat. While you shouldn't deny yourself a meal, there should be plenty of time to eat and spend time in your corner.

If you're really pressed for time, you can use eating as your quiet corner activity. Most of us talk, read, or work as we eat lunch, mindlessly feeding ourselves, paying no attention at all to the activity of eating. One quiet corner you could gain during the day is to close your office door, turn off the radio, turn off the phone, and pay attention to the ritual of eating. Do nothing else. Just eat. Think about your meal and how it tastes; chew mindfully, savoring each bite. Relaxation and satisfaction will be the rewards of this truly rich quiet corner that's open to all of us.

If you're allowed time in the middle of the day to do more than just eat, you can add yet another quiet corner at this time. You could continue sitting quietly in your office; you could walk to a nearby park, taking your lunch with you, or to a holy place, you could take a walk each day in a different direction, exploring the surrounding neighborhoods. No matter where you end up, remember to breathe, especially once you've found your quiet corner.

Environment

*A*s you search for your quiet corner your world will begin to expand and you'll notice things that have been around all along. The empty lot on the corner teeming with wildflowers or the morning church bells may enter your consciousness for the first time.

What is your most receptive sense? Are you distracted and annoyed by unnaturally loud noises? Do you feel your body relax when at the ocean? If so, be on the lookout for an especially silent spot. Do you notice a friend's perfume? Do you volunteer to mow the lawn so that you'll be the first to enjoy the smell of freshly cut grass? Your sensitivities can direct you as you proceed in selecting a corner or two. Perhaps your local park has a bed of roses you can park yourself next to so as to satisfy your visual and olfactory senses. If you loved the stillness of libraries as a child, you might try your neighborhood library for a hushed environment. Create your own environment and include elements that speak directly to you.

There are certain times of the day that imbue almost any place with a sense of holiness. It's the place in time that becomes special. For instance, sunrise or sunset can create an atmosphere that exists at no other time. Even special places have a time during the day when they become enhanced and more special than usual. Be on the lookout for this magical confluence of time and place.

As you continue to observe your surroundings and register your responses to their stimuli your choices will become endless. Remaining alert and aware will broaden your reach. As you open up, so will your world.

Find the Time

$\mathcal{D}$esire is the only requirement necessary to find the time. But find the time we must. Otherwise all intention of finding a quiet corner will remain in our heads as just another good idea. Probably one-quarter of my memory bank was filled with such notions— creative ideas that sat idly by waiting for me to take some action. Little by little, though, as I spend time in my quiet corner (one idea I had a strong enough desire to liberate), I am examining each of these old ideas, resurrecting some, quietly laying others to rest—doing some housecleaning of my crowded mind.

If you feed your desire to spend some time in your own quiet corner you will find the time. Ten minutes here, twenty minutes there. Before you know it, as you get back in touch with yourself and your mind begins to clear, you'll look forward to the fifteen minutes at the end of your workday that you've set aside for yourself. And you'll begin to find other chunks of time waiting for you.

Clichés stand the test of time because of the truth nestled in them. One cliché comes to mind here: "Where there's a will, there's a way." You could also say, "Where there's desire, there's time for a quiet corner."

Solitude

*I*f you're unaccustomed to spending time alone, it will take some time to adjust to the idea and then to the experience of aloneness. Solitude need not be lonely. In fact, as you learn how to spend your time, a richness will develop and the issue of being alone will fade away. You'll become absorbed in your activity, and the outside world will cease to exist. Outside pressures will quiet down, and the demands put on you by yourself and others will subside. When you return to your world, you'll have a fuller appreciation of the people in your life, and more love in your heart.

You might flinch at the idea of spending time alone. Perhaps your memories of time spent alone are sad ones associated with loneliness. Or maybe you're the type who loves to be surrounded by people, and when no one's around, the TV or radio will be on just for the company. Instead of thinking your quiet corner will take you away from others, think of being alone in your quiet corner as a means of bringing you closer to the people in your life. This outlook might make your quiet corner easier to face at first. After some time, when you realize the truth of this, you'll settle down and your resistance will gradually disappear.

The End of the Day

$\mathscr{P}$ut the kids to bed. Prepare for the next day in the usual manner. Then settle down to spend some time in your quiet corner. This period, after the rest of your world has retired for the day, is another perfect time to create a corner. This time of day has its own unique character, and delaying your bedtime slightly will give you a chance to experience it.

The energy in the air quietens in the late evening. A stillness that exists at no other time of day hangs about. There's no need to artificially create quiet. It is waiting for you. Take advantage of it. Even if you have the energy to spend only a few minutes with yourself at this time, it is enough. Simply sit quietly and reflect on your day. Breathe in the calm that surrounds you. Think of nothing. Just breathe. As you review your day, let go of any resentments that might have come up that day. Don't blame yourself or others for difficulties; simply resolve to do better tomorrow. This is the time to nurture yourself and allow the pervasive calm to work its miracle.

It's Your Life

Some people believe that if we make a mess of this life, we'll have another chance to get it right in the next one. Others believe that we have but one life and don't get another chance. Still others believe that we'll be rewarded or punished in the afterlife for our behavior in this one. Whatever you believe is true about your future, you would probably agree that all we can be completely sure of is the present moment. This is it!

Here you are, in this life, in your life, in this moment. Why not do the best you can with what you have now? Treating yourself well in the present rewards you and the people around you immediately. If the rewards extend beyond this moment, so much the better. A quiet corner will be the perfect nurturing ground for reaping the rewards of your life, now or later.

If You Think You Already Spend Too Much Time Alone

There's a thin line between solitude and isolation, between solitude and loneliness. The quality of the time spent alone separates the one from the other. We are social animals. We need the company of other people. Too much time spent alone can be unhealthy, especially if we dwell on the fact of our aloneness. But no time spent alone in our own company can also lead to a feeling of crushing aloneness.

Balance is crucial as you decide how much time to spend in your quiet corner and when. Don't cut yourself off from the world. If you feel cut off, perhaps you could spend some time redressing that. Use your time alone to create imaginative solutions to your isolation. Once you do, the character of your alone time will change. Your loneliness will diminish and you will begin to value your time alone as never before. You will use your time more productively and you will cross that thin line into harmony.

Procrastination

The effort that many of us put into not doing something or the time we spend thinking about doing something can be extremely stressful and anxiety-producing. If you procrastinate, you probably worry about all the time you're wasting as you think about getting started. You probably don't waste as much time as you think you do, but this tendency to worry can make anyone feel harried and rushed. Our society has developed such a fevered pitch in relation to time that busyness is the expected mode of behavior. Time should not be wasted—after all, there's precious little of it. While this attitude can drive us into a whirlwind of doing, doing, doing, we sometimes are caught on the treadmill, rushing to nowhere.

If you find yourself worrying about the time you're wasting or if you feel as if you're rushing and yet not actually doing anything, take a moment to breathe and consider your position. Are you actually procrastinating or are you simply mulling over your approach? A certain amount of mulling is necessary before settling down and doing a project. Observe your patterns and decide how much of your thinking time is wasted and how much of it is necessary and constructive. Then do the things you have to do and use some of your quiet corner time as mulling time.

As you take some steps toward finding a quiet corner, you

may feel some guilt pangs. The voices in your head may tell you that you could be *doing* something with this time. Why not use this time, since you've found it, in a constructive way? Why waste it on being quiet? Indeed, if you're an extremely busy, goal-oriented person—aren't we all to some extent?—you will probably encounter this resistance each time you visit your corner. Even after your search begins, some time has passed, and you're practiced in the art of your quiet corner, you may continue to imagine that you're wasting time. Don't let this interference win out. Keep in mind that we're all conditioned to think this way and only diligence and time will change this pattern. As you begin to experience the enormous rewards of your quiet corner, collect them, and refresh your mind with these memories each time you encounter the waste-of-time bogeyman.

Spending / Saving Time

*W*e are a culture obsessed with time—how much we have or how little we have. We are also under the illusion that we have time to spend or save as we choose. But as the saying goes, time waits for no one. Time just is. It is there whether we are or not and whether or not we pay it attention.

When you first contemplate the idea of a quiet corner, pay no heed to the notion that you have no time to spend there. And once you free up some space in your busy life for this venture, try not to be influenced by the notion that reserving time is enough. This time will simply disappear if not used. You must continue to find the time each time. While at first it will seem like a Herculean effort, once you begin this process you will notice that time is not what you are manipulating. It is not an outer force that you must control. With time, you will notice that it is your attitude toward time, rather than time itself, that you have been adjusting all along.

And once you admit that you might have such an attitude toward time and that it might be interfering with your growth, you will be able to see how this attitude carries over into many areas of your life and colors your particular perspective on things. How you define events and new experiences will determine whether you see them as roadblocks or opportunities. Ask yourself what a silent retreat means to you. Do you immediately balk at the idea and imagine a time of solitary confinement? Or do you see it as an opportunity to explore your inner self? What about fasting? Is this just another word for starving yourself or is it a means to purify your body? Continue to question your attitudes and work first on your time attitude. Once you adjust this and begin to spend some time in your quiet corner, you can use that time to reflect on some of your other attitudes and how they might be holding you back.

Quintessential Time

*S*can your memory bank. What sorts of experiences are stored there? More than likely, you've probably retained those life events that are significant to you in some way. Your normal day-to-day life experiences probably don't qualify for safekeeping. Perhaps you have certain special accomplishments and achievements stored away—graduations and awards ceremonies, competitive sports events. And that overseas trip you took with your special friend or your summer camp buddy may be locked away in your heart and mind. No doubt there's some trauma and tragedy mixed in as well—a broken heart, the death of a loved one. While some of these memories may be painful to look at, each one changed your life in some way and carries with it a lesson about you and your world.

The time you spend in your quiet corner is likely to become significant enough that you will remember much of it years from now as quality time spent. As you learn how to use this time, you will discover valuable information about yourself that will serve you in your everyday life. You will see yourself—the good and the bad—as never before, and you'll learn significant, memorable lessons that will qualify for your memory bank. You might also clean house a little, make peace with the memories that haunt you, and get rid of those that have served their purpose. A little quiet corner time spent each day guarantees something worth remembering.

Breathe

*A*s the days pass, you will have begun to practice your breathing and homed in on a quiet corner or two. You can now begin to extend your breathing practice. Once you settle into your corner, sit down in a comfortable, relaxed position. You can sit on cushions on the floor or sit upright in a chair. The important thing is to have your spine erect so that your breath will flow freely, naturally, and comfortably. Whether you choose the floor or a chair, it is a good idea to prop a small cushion under your buttocks so that you almost feel as though you're tilting forward. This will straighten your spine, and as you get used to this position, it will feel more comfortable than normal sitting.

When you're relaxed and comfortable, begin to concentrate on your breathing. As before, breathe slowly and deeply. Count each exhalation until you count ten breaths. Then begin again and count to ten. Continue—and continue. If it makes it easier to stay with the count, count each inhalation and each exhalation up to ten and then begin again. Each time you enter your quiet corner and practice this breathing exercise, lengthen the time you spend doing it. If you lose track of your count, simply return to one and begin again. If you find that your mind drifts and you are way beyond ten, simply stop and begin again. Your mind will not want to cooperate at first. But as you practice, your mind will quit resisting and settle down into the breath. You will gain immediate rewards from this practice. If you can sit and practice this breathing for ten, twenty, or thirty minutes, the rewards will multiply. You will achieve a calm that you never thought possible. The noise in your head, which was loud and overwhelming at first, will subside. You will leave your quiet corner a quieter person.

Facing Your Quiet Corner

*C*hances are that once you contemplate the idea of spending time quietly alone, you will feel some anxiety. It's perfectly normal, if accustomed to a fast-paced and constantly moving world, to become disoriented when the movement stops. Even the thought of jumping off can raise some fears. Our mind can be our own worst enemy.

The antidote for this is slow, deep breathing. Conscious breathing is an instant, magical cure and instills in us the courage to move forward. Its power to transform us and lessen our fear should convince us to never take anything for granted.

When anxiety takes hold of you as you contemplate facing your quiet corner, simply resort to concentrated breathing and you will be able to take your next step. Breathe, breathe, and breathe some more.

Resistance

The garbage needs to be emptied. The cat's claws need to be clipped. The back closet needs cleaning, and that letter to Aunt Flo simply can't wait any longer. As you approach, or think about entering, your quiet corner, you may be distracted by the need to do something else. Don't be surprised by this. There are many diversions waiting for you that often look more inviting than your corner. This is your mind resisting the idea of quieting down and facing yourself.

Your fears feed your imagination, and your quiet corner suddenly looms large, loud, and threatening. Anything but facing your corner and yourself becomes attractive. The longer you resist entering your quiet corner, the more powerful the force not to becomes. All it takes is a step over that line of resistance. Once you commit yourself, make the decision, then take that step—quiet ensues almost at once. You begin to wonder what all the noise was about. You relax and soon find yourself comfortable and peaceful in your quiet corner.

This resistance to enter your quiet corner may never disappear completely. You may meet it each time. Sometimes it may fool you and appear as a legitimate distraction. Keep your resolve and try not to be swayed. Simply acknowledge the resistance, accept it for what it is, and push through it into your quiet space, leaving it behind.

41

Energy

*F*inding the time. Dealing with avoidance and fear. Pushing through the resistance. Learning to breathe again. You might be asking yourself, why bother? It all sounds like so much effort. Where will the energy come from, and is it worth it?

This is the Catch-22 of putting a quiet corner in your life. In order to get there you do have to expend some energy. You get more back than you spend, but then you have to spend it for your next quiet corner. And so on and so on.

But. As you continue the practice of your quiet corner, the quality of your energy will change and you will always have the energy you need. When you carry over your quiet corner practices—breathing, mindfulness and so forth—into other areas of your life, your energy will be constant and strong. You will rarely run out, and any loss of sleep you experience as a result of your quiet corner will more than be made up for in the energy gained. In order to get energy you must spend a little, and once a quiet corner practice becomes a cornerstone in your life you will not recall how you once struggled to find the energy to get there. In fact, you will someday get to the point where you will retreat to your quiet corner in order to replenish your energy reserves.

The Paradox—So Easy, Yet So Hard

You need no special skills to face a quiet corner. No special talents. No special brainpower. Each one of us has the raw material necessary. Desire is a requirement, but if you're reading this you already have that. Simply set some time aside, choose a spot, get comfortable, breathe, and voilá—a quiet corner! Sounds easy. So why is it so hard?

Fear. Of the unknown, of ourselves, of change. The idea of being quiet and alone with ourselves is a foreign one. Many of us are more comfortable in situations where we know what to expect, even if it's painful, than in situations where there's uncertainty. But life is uncertain, and even if we think we know how something will turn out, we don't.

If you push through the fear and concentrate on the easy aspects of your quiet corner, once you're in there you'll be able to deal with the hard aspects. If you don't take the risk, you'll never know. But if you do, once you're on the other side of your fear, you will be able to look at and understand it. Use the fear as your teacher, and the lessons you learn will be useful and everlasting. You may find that after a quiet corner session your fear has abated and your willingness to embrace change is strong. As a matter of fact, strength to face many areas of your life might surface, as facing your fear will give you courage to move into other previously scary territory. So dance with your fear and glide into new and exciting personal exploration arenas.

Who's Looking?

Awards ceremonies, diplomas, honor rolls, first-place medals, promotions, pay raises, scholarships. These are just some of the ways that our society recognizes and rewards achievement. It is often what motivates us, the carrot at the end of the stick. When we search for a quiet corner, there is no tangible carrot awaiting us. And we're not being graded. No one is watching.

We enter the stream alone and report back only to ourselves. The rewards are quiet, subtle ones—no marching bands. When we keep at it, those we love will share in the benefits without perhaps even knowing how or why. And there's no need to share the specifics of your transformation with others. Let it be your secret. Let your quiet corner be a place where you commune with yourself and, if it works for you, with your higher power. No one is watching. But everyone gains.

Acceptance

Through each step of the process of finding, facing, and using a quiet corner, you will learn a great deal about yourself. The first thing you might learn is how you deal with process. While there is some instant gratification in three-part, three-breath breathing, most of the lasting and strengthening rewards of spending time in a quiet corner are gradual and subtle. An acceptance of this process will be necessary in order to enjoy the long-term promises.

Your individual approach and your idiosyncracies will become apparent throughout the process. Remember that there is no right way to do this. Accept your way. If you circle your corner in procrastination before finally entering, accept this as your process. If you dip in and out before settling down, accept this as your process. Whatever your approach is, if it works for you, it's the right way.

Some of what you learn may not sit well and you may practice denial as you struggle toward perfection. But we are in process here, not perfection. Many Native American works of art contain intentional flaws because of the belief that only the Creator can create perfection. Keep this in mind as you sit in the process. And practice acceptance.

Projection

The anticipation of an event is often more thrilling than the event itself. This knack that we all seem to have, of projecting, fantasizing, and distorting reality, may sometimes serve us well. But it can also be our undoing. The idea of spending time alone may elicit feelings of both fear and pleasure. We may look forward to time alone as a welcome and refreshing reprieve from our hectic lives. But if we take this thought one step further, we may feel some dread about this unstructured time alone, fearing that we won't know what to do. And this might just keep us from facing our quiet corner.

The simple answer here is this: just don't think ahead. While this may sound impossible, it's not. While it may not be easy, it is simple. Go ahead and reserve your quiet corner time; then relax and don't think about it again until you're in it. Trust yourself. You'll know what to do. Keep the pleasure and the terror at bay. Simply plan to be in your quiet corner without attaching emotion to the experience before the experience begins.

As you move along your quiet corner path and learn not to project about your time spent there, you can transfer this new skill to other areas of your life. Plan your next vacation, but try not to predict exactly how you'll spend your days or how you'll feel at the end of the trip. Simply make your plans and show up for the magic. Do likewise with other social and work events. Show up prepared, but be ready for anything. If you can do this, you will avoid disappointment and you will be open and available to the wonder of life and its magnificent treats and surprises. As you perfect this skill, you will see how your previous behavior was limiting you and how this new behavior opens your world to an abundance of possibilities. While this is all very exciting, remember not to get excited until the excitement is upon you. Then it will be truly glorious and real.

Faith

*E*ven if you take all the suggestions in this book, you are bound to come up against a wall now and then. You may sometimes wonder exactly what you are doing, as nothing seems to be happening. And at times throughout this quiet corner process (there's that word again!) you may question your everything. At such times you will need to reach into your heart and grab hold of some faith—faith that the process works, faith that you are on the right path, faith that all is not for naught.

Turning to faith to get you through the rocky moments will be especially critical as you begin this process. Further along the path, as you build up your experiences, you will be able to identify these illusionary roadblocks for what they usually are—annoying distractions that have no base in reality. But in the beginning, faith is often necessary to push you through. And faith will come in handy as you continue your journey when all that you believed is called into question. Turning to faith early on in the process makes it much more accessible later on.

The word "faith" has been so closely associated with religion over the years that in some circles it has a negative connotation. If you are included in one of those circles, try for a moment to disassociate faith from religion. Think of faith as a heart thing that has nothing to do with your brain. Try to let go of the old meaning and don't attach any new meaning to it. Just try to feel it. First, challenge yourself and have faith in your ability to follow the quiet corner path. From there it's easy to transfer that faith to the process and know that as long as you proceed faithfully, you will be in sync with the process and the process will not fail you. Keep faith in your heart and you won't even have to think about it.

Let Your Breathing Guide You

*L*isten to your breath all along the way. As you proceed with finding a quiet corner, and each time you settle into one, allow your breath, not your brain, to guide you. As thoughts rise, identify and accept them as thoughts and let them float away. Just breathe. As you breathe and concentrate on each breath, become aware of the source of your breath.

Lie on your back on the floor with your arms gently relaxed at your sides, palms up. Relax and breathe into your lower abdomen. As you inhale, notice your stomach rise. As you exhale, notice it fall. If your breath is stuck in your throat or chest, try sending it down to your abdomen. Place one palm on your stomach so that you can feel the motion of your breathing. If you've ever watched a young baby breathe you will know how smooth, natural, and unhindered breathing can be. Try to breathe like a child. Each time you practice your breathing, come back to this exercise until this way of breathing becomes natural again in any position.

While it may take some time and practice to soften and deepen your breathing, turn to it at any point and use it as your guide. If your mind is clouded with too many thoughts and your brain is in overdrive, turn it all over to your breath and allow this natural rhythm to sort it all out. Take yourself out of the picture. Just breathe. If you are in your quiet corner and don't know what to do, listen to your breath and stop trying to make a decision. Let your breath do it for you. Give up that responsibility. Just breathe.

Quiet Corner Walking

Do you jump in your car to go two blocks to the corner grocer? Do you hop on a bus to travel a mile to the movies? Do you drive to the train station in the morning rather than walk the half mile? If so, these are perfect opportunities to grab some quiet time, and get some physical exercise as well.

Give yourself a little extra time and set out walking to your destination. Choose a posture and pace that feel comfortable and that suit your body. Begin walking slowly, inhaling and exhaling deeply as you do. Concentrate on your breathing as you walk. As your concentration deepens, you will become keenly aware of, but not distracted by, your surroundings. By softly focusing your eyes about three feet in front of you, your concentration will improve.

Try this walking exercise once or twice and observe your state of mind when you reach your destination. I find that I'm relaxed and yet alert at the same time. Colors are deeper, images are sharper, sounds are crisper. I have more patience in the slow-moving bank or grocery line.

There are many occasions during the day to practice quiet walking. Walk the stairs at work rather than take the elevator; practice a version of quiet walking as you walk the dog. Use your imagination. And remember to breathe.

Is This Meditation?

The dictionary offers a simple definition of "meditation" but our minds tend to embellish the definition and make it into something mysterious and forbidding. There are many different types of meditation, and the external form of any one of them may be the image we carry in our minds of what meditation is. This image may scare us off from even contemplating contemplation. Some people use words to meditate, some use images, and some use sounds. Many people also meditate with closed eyes, but I find that this can cause drowsiness and encourage daydreaming. For our purposes, let's define our quiet corner practice simply as "concentrated breathing with eyes gently open." Simple. And effective.

As you begin to sit quietly in this fashion, breathing deeply, you may want to introduce an image or a sound into your practice to deepen your concentration, but this is not necessary. If all you ever do in your quiet corner is sit quietly with eyes open and breathe, you can consider yourself meditating.

Light a Candle

Since you will be sitting in your quiet corner breathing deeply with your eyes gently open, you might want to observe the source of light in your corner. If you find yourself there in the morning and your windows are enough to allow in natural light, open wide your shades and notice how the light changes as time passes. If you're there in the middle of the day, you might want to draw the shades to dim the light. Here also you can observe shifts in the light patterns. Drawing the shades is a way to soften the mood in the room and create an atmosphere that is unique to that time of day.

If your quiet time falls after the sun sets, light a candle, or light many candles. Candlelight can be especially soothing and mood-creating. There's something about the flickering light and the color generated that softens and changes your everyday surroundings. This will alter your perspective. And this is the true reason you need quiet corner time. By lighting candles at the beginning of your quiet corner period you will be marking off this time as special. As you sit quietly in your corner filled with candlelight, cherish each moment and consider it perfect.

Burn Some Incense

The smell of cotton candy brings to mind amusement parks and the thrill of being a child. The smell of wet fallen leaves brings the sad memory of summer's end and the happy one of school's beginning. For most of us our sense of smell is rather strong and peculiar to our individual tastes and personalities. Unpleasant smells may dampen our mood while pleasant ones bolster it.

When I set aside time to spend in my corner, I first light some incense. The smell signifies to me that my quiet time has begun. I'm less likely to allow distractions. I determine how much incense will burn in the time I've allotted myself, freeing me to concentrate on my quiet corner activity without consulting my watch. I make a ritual of lighting incense every time I visit my corner, and the smell of it has an immediate calming effect. Each time I smell incense I am reminded of my quiet corner. This smell has been added to the others in my sense memory, and it always invokes quietude.

Buy an incense burner or simply burn your incense in a favorite cup or small bowl. When you begin, you will need some pebbles or some salt to stand the incense upright. As ashes accumulate, use them to stick the incense into, and after each session in your quiet corner smooth out the ashes so they're neat and ready for your next visit.

Beginning and ending my quiet corner time with the incense ritual gives a frame to that time and gives me an activity that expresses my commitment to spending time with myself.

Entertain Yourself

$\mathcal{W}$e are constantly being barraged with entertainment. The music in restaurants, the video images in many stores, highway billboards, computer games and networks, TV talk shows, TV nightly news and magazine shows, late night TV shows, movies, videotapes, video games, magazines. The list is endless. All of these forms of entertainment compete for our time. And there's never enough time to do it and see it all despite the pressure put on us to do so. Small wonder why so many of us crave some quiet time but aren't quite sure how to use it.

The first step is to lessen the amount of outside stimulation that enters your world. You do have some control over this. Think carefully about what you allow into your life. Before you turn on the radio or TV, make a conscious decision about it. Think about what you want to hear and see, and proceed with that in mind. If you notice yourself mindlessly tuning in or half listening to a program, spend that time in your quiet corner instead. Think of it as self-entertainment.

If you wake every morning to the sound of your favorite radio station blaring in your ear, you might consider using a gentler alarm and rising in silence. Wait at least a half hour before you tune in to the news and weather as you prepare for your day. If you read the paper every morning, perhaps taking a break from the printed news every other day would free up some quiet time. Try this for a week or two to determine how much important news you actually miss. If you turn the evening news on when you get home from work and leave the TV on as entertainment, you might try watching an hour less each day. Again, decide at the end of a week if you've missed anything worthwhile. Slowly but surely you will replace much of your leisure time with quiet corner time and be stimulated in a way that can never be achieved by external stimulation.

Consult the Child in You

Some of my warmest childhood memories are of spending summer evenings on the back stoop with the neighborhood kids and all our mothers. We had had our baths and were in our pajamas. We couldn't romp around too much because we were already cleaned up for bed, but we found many ways to have fun. And our clean bodies and cotton pj's made us feel safe and comforted with our mothers chatting in the background.

To achieve this feeling as an adult I dress in baggy cotton sweatpants and oversized T-shirts. And as much as possible I walk around barefoot, especially in my quiet corner.

So as to separate your quiet corner time as much as possible from the everyday—that is, until all of your time is quiet corner time—look to your childhood and incorporate elements into your quiet corner that made you particularly happy back then. Or think of something that you always wanted as a child and incorporate that. Perhaps you might set up a fish tank in your quiet corner space. Or paste stars on the ceiling of your room. Be creative, have fun, and remember to consult with the child in you whenever you make those quiet corner decisions.

Read Quietly Aloud to Yourself

$\mathscr{E}$nter your quiet corner and settle yourself down with some concentrated breathing. Select a favorite story or poem and slowly and carefully read it out loud. You may want to start this exercise by reading aloud a favorite children's story. There's a wealth of material to choose from. If reading out loud at first seems awkward to you, you can pretend to be reading to a child. Or you can read to yourself as if you are the child and either relive the experience of being read to or experience the pleasure for the first time. You could also read passages from this book, especially the ones on breathing, to remind yourself to breathe. One of the benefits of reading aloud is that in order to do it you must breathe, and as you proceed, your breathing will become deeper and smoother.

If you want to share your quiet corner time with another person, you could take turns reading to each other. Beginning and ending this time with a shared period of silence could lend a sacredness to the time. It would also introduce you to the power of sitting in silence with another, breathing human being—one who shares your interest in this process.

Try to breathe from your abdomen, as you read aloud. Take the words from deep within you and let your breath carry them forward and out into the world.

Practice, Practice, Practice

Whatever gain you get from your quiet corner today may carry through to tomorrow, but it will begin to fade if you don't continue the practice of taking quiet corner time. And while the effects of this practice are cumulative, you must practice daily in order for this to be so. As with anything worthwhile, your quiet corner experience gets better with practice and time.

There will be many days when retreating to your quiet corner will seem to take more effort than you think it's worth. Go there anyway. There may be days when you feel stuck and your quiet corner seems more a burden than a luxury. Go there anyway. Even if you feel you can spare only ten minutes some days, that's enough. If you wait for the perfect time, the perfect motivation, and the perfect setting, you may never get there. Keep going there and practice your practice.

Make It a Habit

*I*f you're like most people, you probably have a set way of doing most things, whether it's what you eat for breakfast or how you wash your body during your shower. More than likely you have established certain habitual ways of doing things that you rarely even notice or give much thought to. While the breathing practices, the search for quiet corners, and the mindful approach to life suggested in this book, are all meant to break these habitual patterns and allow you to see your world from a different angle, your tendency to establish habits can serve you well as you begin this journey.

Decide that putting a quiet corner in your day is as crucial to your survival and well-being as your daily shower or evening meal. Force yourself to include time for yourself every day until quiet corner time becomes a habit and your equilibrium gets thrown off if you miss a day. Once this time becomes a necessary part of your life you can use it to review all your habitual patterns and break them down one by one. Making your quiet corner a habit will help you to see and perhaps change all your other habits.

Cultivate Your Own Distinct Style

There is no Absolute Right Way to do any of this. Everything here is but a suggestion, an outline for you to use as you proceed along your unique path toward awareness. The intention for each of us in this process is to wake up the spirit. And just as we all have a different internal clock, we also all have different sensitivities. Our individual moods are wont to change, and the perfect approach today might be a disaster tomorrow. So take from this book what works for you and leave the rest. Build on this structure to construct your own quiet corner system.

As you create your quiet corner and spend more time there, your self-awareness will heighten. Your likes and dislikes will become more apparent, yet you won't judge yourself. You'll simply begin to accept the various elements—good and bad—that make you you. Use this knowledge as you cultivate your quiet corner experiences. It is in your quiet corner that you can experiment with new aspects of yourself and bury old ones that no longer work for you. Don't be afraid to entertain the suggestions of others, but don't lock yourself into someone else's vision. Spread your wings in your quiet corner so that you will fly into the world with your personal style in full feather.

Ritual

$\mathcal{D}$oing the same thing over and over in the same way and manner can often lead to stupefaction. For instance, if we perform the same tasks every morning as we prepare for our day and follow the same route to our destination, we might zone out and forget whether we actually mailed those bills and letters we thought we were carrying when we left the house. Or if we sit in front of the TV every night, we might wonder at week's end where the time went and feel dulled and listless. This may be confused with ritual, but it is just our habitual patterns at work.

Ritual is something else entirely and can be invigorating and liberating. Ceremonial ritual can imbue life with order and purpose. When we observe certain rituals being performed, whether in the secular or the religious world, we may not always understand the meaning but we can probably appreciate the beauty. If we bring some of this ritual into our quiet corner, we can mark this time as special. Lighting candles or incense, reading the same passage each time, beginning and ending the time with a favorite prayer or song—even these small touches after a while will carry great significance. And if we ritualize our quiet corner time we will find freedom within the ritual to move beyond the ordinary and begin to gain a new understanding and appreciation of our world. Continuing this practice beyond your quiet corner and introducing ritual into all your activities will make even a mundane chore such as washing the dishes a remarkable event.

Keep It Yours

No two minds work alike, no two bodies react the same, and no one else has your individual stamp, so try not to compare your experiences and progress in your quiet corner with anyone else's. Since we seem to attract people with similar interests, some of your friends and family members may also be on the quiet corner path. It is often necessary and helpful to compare notes and to share experiences, but be careful to avoid thinking that others are doing everything right and you are doing it wrong, or vice versa. That is impossible. You have your style, they have theirs, and both styles are perfect.

Also, while it is helpful and advisable to take suggestions from others who have been on the path longer, it is not necessary to force yourself into something that doesn't fit. At the same time, keep in mind that all of this will seem awkward and uncomfortable at first, so try to avoid using this awkwardness as an excuse not to change. Discomfort is different from twisting yourself into someone else's pattern. You will quickly be able to discern the difference. You will know what is right for you. You will learn to accept your way and respect the ways of others. Your way is not the only way, but it is yours.

Sharing

*I*f you have friends or family members who are also committed to finding a quiet corner, you may want to start a group quiet corner. This shared experience is unlike any other and will teach you much about the world and your place in it. The group experience will also help you if you are having trouble with self-discipline.

You might want to begin each group session with a prayer, song, or chant that you all recite together out loud. Or you might want each person to light a candle or a stick of incense before you begin. Or you might choose to have one person each time share an individual quiet corner experience that you all can concentrate on. Perhaps the members could take turns orchestrating a session. Or you could all agree beforehand how the session should evolve. Try to keep it simple, though.

Most important, be sure that some of this quiet corner time is just that, quiet. Decide to spend a certain amount of this time sitting in complete silence. You could arrange for a small bell to ring signifying the beginning and end of this silent period so that no one will have to watch the clock and everyone will feel free to let go. With two or more people sitting together in silence, breathing and concentrating, amazing things will begin to happen. Extend the silent period each time you meet as a group. First try ten minutes, then twenty, and so on. The longer you sit together in shared silence, the greater the rewards. Sharing in this way will put you in touch with each other as nothing else will, and this experience could alter your view of the universe.

Prayer

When you step into your quiet corner you might want to formally acknowledge that there is a force at work in the world that you have no control over. Whether you believe this force to be God or physics or nature or your higher self, it doesn't matter. If you've given this some thought you will probably agree that there is something bigger and more powerful than you in the universe even if you don't have a name for it. One way to invite this force into your world is with prayer. And beginning and ending your quiet corner time with prayer frames that time with reverence.

A prayer can be viewed simply as an invocation to a force outside yourself or deep within you that will unlock your heart and open it to a fresh outlook. These invocations, inspirational sayings, or prayers can be found in many places. The many and varied religions and cultures of the world and our greatest thinkers and spiritual leaders have provided a plethora of prayers for you to choose from. A trip to your local bookstore will immediately reveal the rich source of inspiration available to you. As you make your selections, you might want to read a different prayer each time you visit your quiet corner. As you discover new prayers, there may be one or two that you commit to memory so that you can use them during the day when you find yourself in a jam, or when you feel tense. Silently reciting a prayer over and over often relieves tension and will help guide you through the rough spots.

The beauty of the language in most prayers is often enough to wake me up and alter my perspective. I begin to view the world in a new light and become ready for any challenge. My quiet corner experience is profoundly moving when prayer is a part of it.

Insomnia

Tossing and turning all night. Thoughts of what didn't get done today and what must get done tomorrow. Misery over the breakup of a relationship. Grief over the death of someone dear. Worry about a sibling or child. Too many bills to pay. And on and on.

No one is exempt from troubles, and we've all had our share of sleepless nights. But instead of lying in torment, consider this an opportunity to retreat to a quiet corner. You won't be getting any sleep anyway, and the rest of your world is down for the night, so not why spend some extra time in your corner? You can face some of the demons that are squawking at you, and you'll be less tired in the morning for your efforts.

When you reach your quiet corner, keep the lights down low or use candles. Sit on some cushions on the floor and be sure you're warm enough. Make your corner cozy and comfortable. Now breathe. As each disturbing or obsessive thought rises, breathe. Continue breathing deeply with your eyes gently open. See the fear attached to the worry. Breathe. Notice your own attachment to that person. Breathe. Yesterday is over, tomorrow not yet here. Breathe. You are right now in a warm place, secure for the moment. Continue breathing as your thoughts slow down. Perhaps some insight will be yours as you proceed and breathe through your worry. You may soon find yourself nodding off, ready for sleep. Breathe a little more before returning to bed and continue the practice as you lie down. Breathe yourself into a peaceful sleep.

When Things Don't Go Your Way

We all have days, weeks, or even longer periods when we feel stretched to our limit. The least little thing can set us off and cause us to behave in a manner that is unbecoming and perhaps unkind. At times like this we might become inflexible, setting rigid standards for, and expectations of, ourselves and others. Normally, if our train is late or if our child or pet gets sick we would take it in our stride. But there are times when it seems as if the world is actually against us, as if circumstances are conspiring to aggravate us; nothing seems to be going our way. These are especially important times to spend a few moments taking stock.

You might be aware of your behavior and feel there is nothing you can do about it. You shrug it off and decide that it will pass at some point. But there's no need to wait until it passes. Sitting in the negative energy of such times only hurts you and those around you.

One very simple exercise you can do, even though it's the last thing you might think of doing, is smile. If your facial muscles won't cooperate because your frown is winning the fight, simply force your mouth into a smile with your fingers. Even this will begin to change your mood. Breathe as you do this, and allow yourself to feel silly. Continue to push your face into a smile until you feel yourself relaxing and the tension easing. At some point you may even be able to laugh out loud at yourself and your struggle to make everything work the way you want it to work, when you want it to work. The world just doesn't always cooperate. And there is humor in this if you give yourself a moment to see it. So smile when you least expect to and your expectations won't get the best of you.

Turn Bad Situations to Your Advantage

$\mathcal{T}$ake some time along the way to stop and smell the roses."
While this suggestion may be dated and old fashioned, it seems
that collectively we've moved so far from this that the goal has
become all important and the route is but a nuisance. We focus
on the outcome or intention of each event, even a simple chore
or outing. Everyday activities are conducted on automatic pilot
so that much of our day is a blur.

When your path seems littered with obstructions and you
become impatient and irritable, take a moment and observe just
why you are annoyed. Are you at your destination before you
even arrive? The next time you are sitting in traffic, on your way
to some other place, take note of your reactions. Are you disturbed
because you'll be late or because such situations make you feel
totally helpless? Reflect on the why and how of your feelings.
This is a terrific opportunity to take a moment and become more
familiar with yourself. It's also a perfect time to create a quiet
corner. You can't go anywhere, the situation is completely out
of your control, and this is private time you might not otherwise
have found. Breathe deeply and calm down. Enjoy the gift rather
than cursing the misfortune.

Have you ever actually timed the traffic light that won't turn green quickly enough? Next time you're sitting there drumming the steering wheel, breathe deeply a few times and actually time the light. It will seem to change much sooner if you are calm and relaxed than if you are rushed and anxious. Another opportunity for a time-out.

And as you stand in the slow-moving ticket line, talk to your neighbor about the show you are about to see rather than the poor management of the theater. Or, again, spend this found time standing calmly in your quiet corner, and breathe. Your enjoyment of the show and of your day will be much enhanced.

Breathe

*A*s you spend more and more time in your quiet corner, and as your concentration improves, you might begin to notice a few things. First, while the cessation of thought might be your ultimate desire, you won't stop thinking. But you will have more and longer periods with little mind interference. These moments of quiet will prepare you for the onslaught of thoughts that is sure to come. When it does come, try to use your new powers of concentration and fortitude to simply notice these thoughts as thoughts, and then let them go. Try not to latch on to a thought or to continue thinking the thought. Acknowledge that you are having a thought, breathe, and wait for the next one. Don't follow any one thought.

As you sit concentrating on your breathing, detaching yourself from your thoughts, you will become aware of your breath in a surprising and unusual way. You can get to the point where you will notice that your breath is breathing you. *You* are not actually breathing; your breath is breathing. This is a strangely liberating experience and one that's hard to imagine as you read this. But if you continue your breathing, thinking and not thinking, and let your breath breathe you, the experience will be yours.

Singing

*H*ave you ever wondered why most religious ceremonies include songs or chants? Even sports events—a religion to many—begin with the national anthem. Singing is a magnificent form of expression and it has the benefit of being a physically healthful exercise as well.

Once you've settled yourself into your corner by sitting quietly and consciously breathing, slowly begin to chant or sing some passages that you've selected beforehand. Choosing something unfamiliar will force you to concentrate that much harder on each syllable, and this will force other distracting thoughts from your mind, freeing you to concentrate even more. As you sing, become aware of your breathing. Bring each sound up from your abdomen along with your breath. Keeping your spine erect will allow your breath and each sound to flow smoothly.

Experiment with the tempo and volume. For instance, you might want to start off slow and quiet and build up to fast and loud. Once you stop, sit in silence for a few moments and bathe in the stillness. You will probably be more sensitive to the sounds around you: the birds outside your window may sound especially musical and cheerful; the rain on your windows might sound friendly and warm. You might even discover some new sounds around you. Continue breathing. You will find a difference in your breathing practice after singing or chanting. Your diaphragm and your heart will be more open than usual, allowing your silent breathing to work its miracle in your quiet corner.

Calming the Mind

Concentrated breathing, silent sitting, chanting, and sing-ing—all of these are simply techniques to quiet the chatter in our brains so that we can observe our true and natural selves. With so many external stimuli and so much overstimulation in our lives, it's not easy to find the quiet. There may be quiet corner sessions where you never actually find the quiet. Don't be discour-aged. The quiet will come.

And the quiet will bring calmness of mind. And a calm mind will bring calmness of spirit. Within this calm you will be able to look with some detachment at your thoughts and your behav-ior. Your place in the world will become clearer, and confusion will diminish. Answers to vexing problems will become apparent. It is simple but not easy. Just sit still and breathe quietly, and a calm mind will be yours.

Where Is the Mind and Who Is Its Master?

$\mathscr{A}$s you spend more and more time in your quiet corner, breathing and noticing your thoughts, devote a few sessions to concentrating on the source of your thoughts. Where are they coming from? What generates them? Why this particular thought in this particular moment and not another? Be the observer as your mind works.

Distancing yourself from the workings of your mind and the thoughts that arise will enable you to gain some perspective on yourself. Just slowing down and listening to your rhythm will make a difference. Even the simple willingness to do this will have a profound impact on your life.

Your mind may often seem to have a mind of its own. No matter how much you bid it to slow down and be quiet, if it wants to be busy and noisy it will be. As you sit and listen to this noise, ask yourself why it exists. What, other than you, is driving it? The answer may not be readily apparent, now or ever. But in order to gain some serenity in this world it is important to ask the question.

Concentration

Concentrated fruit juice is essentially juice with all the water, a nonessential ingredient, drained out of it. You would not want to drink juice in this pure form, however. Before you can drink it, that nonessential ingredient, water, must be put back in.

Think of meditation and time spent in your quiet corner as a means of removing the nonessential ingredients from your life for a short time. As with the juice, you will at some point discover that nothing is nonessential, but spending some time in concentration is one way to discover this.

There are many different concentration techniques. Experiment with different ones and use the ones that work for you. You might repeat one word over and over in your mind, concentrating on the form, shape, and meaning of that word. Choose a word that means nothing to you; a foreign word might work best. Or focus on an image. Visualize something in your mind or place an object in front of you. Devote all of your attention to this image or object. And don't forget to breathe. Breathing, of course, is another way to concentrate. Count your breaths; simply follow your breath and set your mind fully on it; if you can't concentrate on both the inhalation and the exhalation, concentrate on just a half breath; or simply let your breath breathe, and pay attention. Repeating a phrase over and over in your mind is also a good way to concentrate. Choosing one that brings your attention to the current moment may be most effective.

As your ability to concentrate improves, elements of your life that you once regarded as nonessential and perhaps bothersome will either fade away or become integrated. You will be calmer and much more able to accept the previously unacceptable. The how and why of this process will more than likely remain a mystery. So be it.

Love

*Y*ou may be asking yourself, What does all of this have to do with love? How does love fit in with a quiet corner? If I take myself away from the world every day and sit in a quiet corner by myself, am I not taking time away from others with whom I want to spend time and to whom I want to express love? These are all valid questions, and if you're asking them you're probably ready to hear the answers.

If you are committed to the quiet corner path, every part of your being and every aspect of your life will be affected. The changes will at first seem to be subtle, minor changes. But as time passes, you will learn to accept how profound each one really is. Your quiet corner practice of concentration will increase your awareness, and that in turn will introduce more patience and tolerance into your life. These will determine first how you treat yourself and then how you treat others. As you grow, your ability to feel and express compassion will also grow. As you come to understand yourself and the motives behind your behavior, you will appreciate others more and have an increased capacity to practice unconditional love. Your expectations will not be what they once were, and there will be more room in your life for love as well as more time for it. Taking time out for your daily quiet corner will yield an abundance of love. So begin by loving yourself enough to find your quiet corner, and you will be rewarded with more than enough love. Understanding yourself and others is the key to love. Simply retreat to your quiet corner and breathe.

Progress, Not Perfection

$\mathcal{I}$f you're anything at all like me you hate to settle for less than perfection. This attitude causes endless disappointment and much blaming and finger-pointing. The finger may often point back at you, and it carries enough negativity and judgment to do some serious damage. Let's nip this attitude in the bud before it has the opportunity.

If you gain nothing from this book but the understanding that life in all its aspects is ever-changing, unpredictable, and not controllable by any of us, that's enough. If you slowly but surely come to realize that you are perfect as you are, that's enough. If you decide to introduce some quiet corners into your life, with no expectations, that's enough.

While each one of us, and everything about our lives, is perfect just as it is, very few of us believe this. But if we believe that we are less than perfect, give up the struggle to be perfect, and concentrate on our process—that's perfection. In your quiet corner you can get in touch with this perfection. Know that there you are perfect, that everything is perfect.

When you enter your quiet corner leave your private personal judge outside. As you learn to do without this judge while in your corner, try to exclude it from other areas of your life as well. Before you know it, this judge will be off your shoulder for good. And your progress on the quiet corner path will be less hindered. Perfect.

Drawing and Writing

$\mathcal{I}$f you are visually oriented and tend to learn through seeing, drawing or painting could be one of your quiet corner activities. If drawing is already a part of your life, change the way you draw in your quiet corner so that you might see differently. If you normally draw at a desk, try moving to the floor; if you prefer to draw on an easel, move to a table. If you don't now draw but would like to, experiment with different positions. Bookend each drawing session with silent sitting and concentrated breathing exercises. Use your quiet corner drawing time to focus on whatever thoughts come to you when you sit and breathe. What thought keeps recurring? How does each thought look to you? Draw or paint it so that you can take a closer look. Are you sitting in a pool of anger? What does that look like? Where are you in the picture? As you record your thoughts and feelings try not to edit what you draw. These drawings are for your eyes only. You might even consider destroying them after each session. That would mark a significant beginning in learning the discipline of detachment.

If you think in words rather than images and learn best from the written word, you might want to keep a quiet corner journal. Designate a special notebook and pen to be used only in your quiet corner. Keep them in a safe and private place for you alone.

At some point in this process you may want to share parts of this journal with a trusted friend or adviser, but as you write, pretend that you will be the sole audience. It is much easier to be honest this way.

Each time you enter your quiet corner, sit in silence for a while and do some concentrated breathing exercises while observing your mind. Then write about your thoughts and feelings. Sit quietly again after each writing session so as to observe the difference. The act of writing will often free certain thoughts from your mind that once seemed trapped. It will deflate some feelings to a size that seems manageable. And it will teach you a great deal about yourself.

Freeing your thoughts and feelings through drawing or writing will increase your self-awareness and prepare you to be more observant and tolerant when you are not in your quiet corner.

What Is the Sound of One Hand Clapping?

This Zen question has been used and overused, understood and misunderstood, joked about and taken seriously. At first glance it's a seemingly innocuous and ridiculous question. But it and other such questions can serve a purpose as you spend time in your quiet corner and develop your concentration techniques.

When I was a child the concept of God and eternity both confounded and pleased me. My friends and I never tired of asking questions such as "If God has always been there, when did He first start and who created Him?" We could not wrap our young minds around the notion of beginningless beginning and endless end. My mature mind doesn't have a firm grasp on this concept either, but I feel less frustrated today than I did as a child when contemplating such matters.

Today I love questions such as "If a tree falls in the forest and there's no one around to hear it, does it make any sound?" There may be no answer or many answers to this question; it doesn't matter. I delight in letting the question swim around in my brain. Contemplating such paradoxes takes my mind off my petty everyday troubles and forces me to concentrate.

These questions are excellent tools to use in your quiet corner to improve your concentration. Once you've established your quiet corner and spent some time there practicing your breathing, choose a question that at one time boggled your mind; sit quietly and try to think of nothing else. When you get to this stage in your practice, you might want to seek guidance from someone who has been asking such questions for a long time. But for now, just go to your quiet corner, breathe, and ask yourself, "What is the sound of one hand clapping?"

Who Are You?
Where Did You Come From?
Where Are You Going?

On the face of it these seem to be very simple questions. And you probably answer them often, especially when introducing yourself to new people or when describing your lifestyle. But when you take these questions into your quiet corner and spend some time with them, contemplating their true meaning and all of the possible answers, you will never again see yourself simply as a name, address, and profession, even if you continue to describe yourself in those terms.

Most of us have probably given some thought to what might happen to us after we die. Many of us may even have a firm belief about the afterlife. But how many have considered the question of what happened to us before we were born? If something happens to us after death, why not before birth? While there may be no easy answer and many possibilities, contemplating such a question can be fun and will reveal much about you.

So retreat to the solace of your quiet corner and, when ready, ask yourself who you really are when your name, personality, and labels are stripped away. Ask yourself where you might have come from other than your mother's womb. Think of your death and ask yourself where you will be then. If you have no answers to these questions, or if you have many answers, it's all the same because you may come to some realizations about your life that will matter just by asking the questions. And meanwhile, the disagreement with your boss or the concern about your finances will take on a new texture. Your perception of your place in the world will change. And this is why we ask ourselves these seemingly unanswerable questions in the quiet of our quiet corner.

Relaxing

Lounging in the sun, luxuriating in a hot tub, curling up with a good novel, or fishing in an isolated stream—these are all legitimate and enjoyable ways to relax and recover from the stresses of our fast-paced lives. Most of us relax when we participate in leisure-time activities. However, the relaxation you can achieve from spending time in your quiet corner is different and cannot be compared with these traditional relaxing experiences.

In a quiet corner there often exists some tension—tension from concentrating on your breath or on some frustrating question, tension from observing the thoughts and feelings that cause you discomfort, tension from sitting still and not moving for a short time, tension from confronting yourself and your shortcomings. Even as you read this you might be thinking that picking up a good book and getting lost in the story seems preferable to creating such tension. And some days that is the perfect choice. But the rewards of quiet corner tension are magnificent and certainly better than a sunburn.

There is a simple physical exercise you can do to help you appreciate the partnership of tension and relaxation. Lie on the floor flat on your back with your arms at your sides, palms up. Notice how your body feels against the floor. Where are the tense areas? Raise one leg off the floor, tense your muscles as hard as you can, hold that position, then release the tension, drop your leg back onto the floor, and forget about it. Raise and lower the other leg. Do the same with your arms, hips, torso, shoulders, and head. When you raise your head, squeeze your eyes closed and pucker up your face. Hold the tension for a few seconds before letting go. When you're finished, observe how your body now feels against the floor. Is your body less tense? More relaxed?

When you sit in your quiet corner with tension, you will slowly learn how tension manifests itself in your life and how to ease that tension. The relaxation you will experience after an intense quiet corner session will come in the form of joyous and heightened awareness. You will probably find yourself smiling more. Your mind will be calmer and more relaxed. And as time passes and you develop your particular quiet corner style, you will bring your practice into other activities and learn to relax in all areas of your life.

Sound

*T*rain whistles, church bells, bird songs, ocean waves. We might consider these pleasing sounds. Blaring car horns, jackhammers, loud music, street traffic. We might consider these sounds unpleasant. And when we're irritable or expecting quiet, almost any environmental sound can displease us. So, while this whole book is about "quiet" corners, try not to take that word too literally. Of course, the quieter the better, but don't search for a space that is hermetically sealed and dead silent. In fact, having some extraneous sound enter your quiet corner could be a good thing.

While you're sitting in your quiet corner concentrating on your breath or on some question, your concentration may be interrupted by the sounds of traffic or your neighbors' kids. When this happens, concentrate on the noise instead of becoming irritated by it. Why does the sound disturb you? What can you do about it? What memories or feelings does it stimulate? Before long, you might notice that the noise has abated, or at least it is not as bothersome. You may come to accept such noise as part of your environment and allow it to go on without letting it disturb you. And this will carry over into the rest of your life, teaching you to accept what is happening around you without becoming irritated or trying to interfere.

If you are particularly sensitive to sound, as you sit in your quiet corner dealing with the unpleasant sounds, you may also notice some pleasing sounds that you never noticed or paid attention to before—the fire station whistle marking the hour or the quiet tick of a grandfather clock. If your mind is quiet, your environs will be quiet. And it is in your quiet corner that you can learn to quiet your mind.

Clutter

Clutter interferes with our spiritual progress. When we clutter up our day with endless projects, we have no time left for ourselves. When we allow our physical spaces to become crowded with things, we have to wade through the clutter and sit amid confusion. Notice how calm most museums are: they are simply about the art being shown; there is nothing extraneous.

It's a simple matter to clear away some of the clutter in our lives and avoid creating more. Begin in your designated quiet corner. Diligence in keeping all clutter out of this space will bring rewards. As you spend more time sitting in a clutter-free environment, notice its calming effect. How extraordinary it would be to carry this tranquillity to all areas of our lives. As you go through your day, be mindful of your actions and take care not to create unnecessary clutter. It all begins with awareness, and our quiet corner can be our guide.

Beauty

Whether you have a private corner of your house in which to set up a permanent quiet corner or whether you need to transform your space each time you visit your quiet corner, you will want to have near you something of beauty. An uncluttered space that is visually pleasing with a touch of beauty will set a peaceful and calming mood. This needn't take a large investment, and you might even strive for simplicity. Bring one fresh flower each time and place it in the vase you chose especially for your quiet corner. Or place a large seashell near your candleholder and incense burner. Or hang a nature photograph near where you sit.

If you decide to use your quiet corner time to draw or write, purchase a specially crafted drawing pad or notebook for yourself. You could even wrap it in a silk scarf and tuck it away in a drawer for safekeeping between visits. Include special paintbrushes and pens. Your quiet corner ritual could include unwrapping your notebook and carefully folding the scarf or draping it over a cushion, adding to the beauty of the setting.

The more time you spend in your quiet corner, the more you will notice the beauty around you. You will take great pleasure in arranging flowers, in setting the table. More than likely you will begin to introduce small touches of beauty into all of your personal spaces. Beauty can transform more than just the space. Experiment with it in your quiet corner and let your creativity loose.

Comfort versus Discomfort

Whether it is learned or innate it does seem that we will go to any length to avoid pain. And we will pay almost any price for pleasure and comfort. The odd thing about this is that, if we're paying attention, we come to realize that pain is inevitable and part of the wonder of being human. And we may notice that our searching and grasping for comfort only causes more pain.

To help you understand the discomfort in your life and how you deal with it, you can do a simple exercise in your quiet corner. Choose a comfortable sitting position, cross-legged on the floor or upright in a chair, making sure that your spine is erect and your hands loose in your lap. Begin your breathing exercises and commit yourself to not moving for at least ten minutes. You might want to scratch an itch or blow your nose— try not to. Just sit still. Your leg might fall asleep, or you might want to adjust your posture to ease the strain in your neck. Just sit still. While this may sound like unnecessary torment, if you do this exercise a few times you will learn a great deal about pain and your resistance to it. When you feel some physical discomfort, breathe into that area and relax. Accept that you are in physical pain and will be for a few minutes.

After a few sessions like this you may notice that the pain distracted you from other worries that now seem unimportant.

You may also notice that when you focus on the pain or try to resist it, it intensifies, but if you are able to concentrate on your breathing and accept the pain, it will lessen and may even disappear completely. While you may not experience this immediately, you will eventually. As you continue practicing this exercise, your approach and attitude toward other types of discomfort in your life will change over time. You will find that the less you resist the greater will be your comfort.

Detachment

*P*erhaps the most difficult quiet corner concept to grasp is that of detachment. Yet it is the key to freedom and peace. The most important question you can ask yourself each time you recognize an attachment to something is "How important is it?"

We all form attachments—to people, places, and things. Fear is most likely the underlying force here—fear of not having enough, fear of being alone, fear of failure, and so on. And our attachments, while we think they are normal and warranted, cause us a great deal of pain. We tend to think that we have control over them. Only when we lose them, or as we struggle to hold on to them, do we learn that we never had them in the first place.

Your quiet corner is the perfect place to sit with yourself and review your attachments, what they mean to you and what it would mean to lose them. It is here that you can learn how to detach yourself from the people and things in your life, and to do it with love. And rather than taking you further from the ones you love and making you cold and distant (which is what I once thought detachment was all about) it will bring you closer to people and will teach you how to express love without asking for anything in return. Because you will no longer have an emotional investment in how other people behave, they will gain the freedom to express their love as they need to. And you will learn to love them as they are.

And detaching yourself from the things in your life does not mean doing without or discarding money and nice things. It simply means trying not to make the attainment of such things an end in itself and not allowing them to become all important and the focus of your life. Collect things around you if you must, but be ready to let go of them at any moment with no regrets. Detach from these things before you lose them, and having or not having them will be one and the same.

Focus on the Moment

The ultimate aim of quiet corner practice is to bring ourselves into the present moment, to make ourselves aware of what is happening now—not yesterday or tomorrow, but now. It is to bring us into this moment and keep us here. You may not yet be aware that you are not always living in the moment. But as you continue on the quiet corner path, your awareness will improve. You will notice more readily when you are regressing or projecting. When you do notice, try centering your attention on your breath. Your breath will always help you focus on the present. If you take three deep breaths at such times, you will notice where you are and how you're feeling. Take stock of yourself. Look around you and notice something about your surroundings. Place yourself firmly in the present by taking note of the shoes you're wearing. Take three more deep breaths and notice your posture. Are you holding on to some tension? Breathe into it and let it go. What activity are you engaged in? Bring all of your attention to it and breathe. Don't think about finishing it, just be in it.

Don't Just Do Something, Sit There

*W*hen someone offered this advice to me years ago, I thought I had misheard it. Being a person of action, I would always look for something to *do*, particularly when I was uncomfortable. I've since learned that rather than dealing with the issue at hand, I was running away. I now sit with my thoughts and feelings so as to better understand myself.

When you're feeling sad, lonely, angry, happy, jealous, and so forth, try not to immediately do something about it. Go to your quiet corner and sit down. Breathe your way to understanding. Observe all aspects of your feelings. Try to have compassion for the person who may have inspired the feeling. Write about it. Talk to someone else about it. Think it through.

Whenever you think there must be something more you can do, it may be time to retreat to your quiet corner and extend the time you normally spend there. Use what you've learned along your quiet corner path and build on that. Light your incense, light your candle, sit quietly, and breathe. If you want to push yourself to do something, do it there. Sit for twenty silent minutes, if you can. Regulate your breathing and don't force anything. Just sit. If thoughts come, let them come. And go. If feelings come, let them come. And go. If you experience physical pain, let it be. And let it go. This may be the most difficult thing you can do, because in a sense it is non-doing, but it also may become the most important thing that you do. So if you must do something, just sit there in your quiet corner.

Mindfulness throughout the Day

As you grow along your quiet corner path, practicing your breathing, you will develop the skill to stay in the moment. At first you might ask why this is so important. But as you progress, you will learn that this moment now is truly all there is. And if you are fully awake in this moment, everything is bliss. While this notion may sound like an exaggeration, the promise of it is worth the quest.

The skill to stay in the moment is first learned in your quiet corner. Practice it there and hone it so that you can take it with you and use it outside your quiet corner. Bring it to work with you. As you proceed through your day, pay attention to each task as you are working on it. Try not to sit in a meeting waiting for it to end. Handle each telephone call with your full attention. Bring it home with you. As you prepare supper, avoid thinking of how the food will taste, and just be with the experience of cooking. Take a bath just to take a bath. Bring it into your leisure time. Without worrying about winning, play your tennis game, concentrating on each stroke. Plant the tomato plants without thought of eating their fruit.

The more mindful you become, the less stress you will experience. The more mindful you become, the more time you will seem to have. The more mindful you become, the less you will fear. The more mindful you become, the more acceptance you will have. Begin in your quiet corner and slowly extend this new skill into your whole life. If spacing out in front of the TV or watching a movie is your way to relax, devote your full attention even to these activities and you will be more relaxed than usual. Take your life one moment at a time with your full attention and you will never be disappointed.

Traveling with Your Quiet Corner

Whether you travel for business or pleasure, or both, a trip can be fraught with anxiety, pressure, and stress. Worrying about making a plane connection can ruin your two-hour flight. You will make it or not, and no amount of fretting will change that, so focus your attention on your breath and let the airline take care of the rest.

Lost luggage is one hazard of travel that very few people can accept with equanimity. But if you practice your quiet corner skills as you discover the bad news, you might be surprised at how accepting you can be. Use this experience to observe yourself and how you handle this inconvenience. Will anger and public tantrums change the situation? Will they make you feel better? While almost no one is beyond getting upset, if you bring a little quiet corner onto the scene, your distress can be minimized. If you can find a quiet spot to retreat to for a few minutes, you will return a different person. Breathe and smile.

If you commute to work each day, whether by car or by public transportation, there are likely to be delays. Keep in mind that you are not at the center of the delay; you are not the cause, and you cannot change it. Here again, your quiet corner will come in handy. Sit if you can, breathe consciously, and enjoy the interlude.

So many of us view planes, trains, and cars as simply a means of getting us from one place to another. If you are one of these people, try to change your outlook so that you can then gain the time that you once thought of as wasted, and use it to create more quiet corners in your life. You will no longer view travel time as a necessary evil. You may even begin to look forward to this time, just as you do to your time spent on the other end of the trip. Enjoy the time. It's a gift you didn't know you had.

Imperturbability

*W*hen I first started sitting in my quiet corner and was told to try to detach myself from my thoughts and my feelings, I thought I was being told not to think and feel. I expected to become an unfeeling, unthinking person. But at least, I thought, I would be more enlightened. So I marched on in my search for peace, trying not to feel or think. I didn't get very far and was convinced that I was a failure and would never know peace. But somewhere along the way I learned that detachment from feelings and thoughts doesn't mean we have to stop feeling and thinking. We can no more stop feeling and thinking than we can stop breathing and still be alive and human. I now know it's okay to feel all our emotions and to think all our thoughts. The trick is not to be perturbed by them. Imperturbability is the goal of a quiet corner. And it is achievable. And it is worth the effort. And it may even make us more enlightened.

The big bonus here, once you learn to detach yourself from your thoughts and feelings, is that you will be less and less disturbed by the actions and feelings of others. You will be able to take in your stride anything that comes your way. And the bigger bonus, if you stay on the path and continue retreating to your quiet corner, is that you will also become less judgmental and more compassionate. I can't explain how detaching ourselves from our feelings makes us more able to feel for others, but it does. I will leave the explanation to the mystics. I only know the truth of this and, paradox or not, if imperturbability is possible and will in turn bring you to a joyful connection to your world, you'll be on the path for life.

The Payoff

While it may be admirable to approach any endeavor with no expectations and no need for reward, it's difficult to be human and not want something in return for our efforts. And although all the suggestions in this book are simple, they are not always easy. So I will now dangle a carrot in front of you and describe the rewards of following a quiet corner path. These rewards will not magically appear just by reading this book. You must take the time and expend the effort. But if you do, you will not be disappointed. Simply keep your mind wherever you are and the path will be easier.

A life in balance will be yours. Physically, mentally, and emotionally you will be in harmony with yourself and your surroundings. You will gain some insight into your life and your world. You will achieve clarity of mind. You will smile more and experience more joy. Peace and understanding will be yours. You will want less and be more appreciative of what you have. You will achieve a greater understanding of others and learn to love unconditionally.

All of this is possible if you simply take some time out, sit quietly, and breathe.

Postscript

Your Quiet Corners

*T*here are many suggestions in this book for creating a quiet corner in your life. There is also plenty of room for your creativity to blossom and your imagination to run wild as you develop your own individual quiet corners. I would love to hear from you about your quiet corners. What suggestions do you have for others as they proceed along on this journey? How does your quiet corner look? What elements do you include each time you visit your quiet corner? Do you like your corner to change in appearance regularly or do you feel calmer if it remains quietly the same? What quiet corner experiences would you like to share with others?

Please send your ideas, suggestions, experiences, thoughts, and feelings about your quiet corners to:

> Your Quiet Corners
> c/o Warner Books
> 1271 Avenue of the Americas
> New York, NY 10020